THE CUBAN
MISSILE
CRISIS

P E T E R   C H R I S P

HODDER
Wayland

an imprint of Hodder Children's Books

© 2001 White-Thomson Publishing Ltd

Produced for Hodder Wayland by
White-Thomson Publishing Ltd
2/3 St Andrew's Place
Lewes
BN7 1UP

Series concept: Alex Woolf
Editor: Joanna Bentley
Designer: Derek Lee
Consultant: Scott Lucas, Head of American and Canadian
  Studies, University of Birmingham.
Proofreader: Serena Penman

Published in Great Britain in 2001 by Hodder Wayland, a
division of Hodder Children's Books

The right of Peter Chrisp to be identified as the author of
this work has been asserted by him in accordance with the
Copyright, Designs and Patents Act 1988.

Map illustrations by Nick Hawken

British Library Cataloguing in Publication Data
Chrisp, Peter
  Cuban Missile Crisis. - (The Cold War)
  1. Cuban Missile Crisis, 1962
  I. Title
  973.9'22

ISBN 0 7502 3389 3

Printed and bound in Italy by G. Canale & C.S.p.A., Turin

Hodder Children's Books
A division of Hodder Headline Limited
338 Euston Road, London NW1 3BH

Picture Acknowledgements: The publishers would like to thank
the following for giving permission to use their pictures:
AKG 24, 48, 53, 54; Camera Press *cover*; Christian Science
Monitor 49; Consolidated News Pictures 9;
Bettmann/Corbis 16, 38, 51; James Davies, Eye
Ubiquitous/Corbis 58; Eye Ubiquitous 56; Imperial War
Museum 8; Peter Newark's American Pictures 13, 14, 23,
31; Photri 44; Popperfoto *cover*, 7, 11, 19, 21, 22, 28, 30, 32,
34, 47, 59; Topham Picturepoint 12, 25, 33, 35, 37, 40, 41,
46; United Nations 50; Wayland Picture Library *cover*, 6, 20,
52.

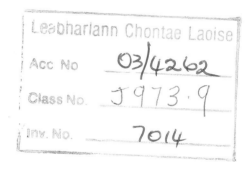

Contents

CHAPTER ONE

On the Brink

OCTOBER 1962 was the most dangerous month in all of human history. The world's two superpowers, the United States and the Soviet Union, stood on the brink of nuclear war. Each had enough weapons to destroy the other, and take half the countries of the world with them.

Their quarrel was over the island of Cuba, just 140 km from the coast of the USA, and an ally of the Soviet Union. Photographs taken by US spy planes showed that the Soviets were building nuclear missile sites in Cuba. Once installation was complete, the missiles would have the range and power to destroy every US city except Seattle, and there would be no defence against them.

US President John Kennedy was determined to get the Soviet missiles out, even if this meant invading Cuba and going to war with the Soviets. Preparations to invade were already under way. The island was surrounded with hundreds of ships, nearly a thousand aircraft and more than 100,000 troops.

Waiting in Cuba was a Soviet army, 42,000 strong, far larger than Kennedy imagined. The troops were armed with tactical nuclear weapons, which they were ready to use.

Range of Soviet Missiles if placed on Cuba

Jet bombers - 1130 kilometres (Atlanta, Miami, Central America)

Medium range ballistic missiles - 1700 kilometres (Washington DC, Houston)

Intermediate range ballistic missiles - 3600 kilometres (nearly all of USA)

◁ This map shows the ranges of different types of Soviet missiles if they were placed in Cuba.

NUCLEAR ALERT

The US armed forces were on alert at 'Defence Condition 2', the highest state of combat readiness short of actual war. All nuclear units were ordered to load their weapons, ready for firing. Long range B-52 bombers took to the air, loaded with nuclear bombs, and circled in readiness. US Polaris submarines headed towards Soviet waters. Each of them carried missiles with more destructive power than all the bombs dropped during World War Two.

President Kennedy was always within a ninety second hail of two military aides carrying a black satchel, nicknamed 'the football'. This held the codes that the President would use to unleash nuclear war. In underground bunkers, officers of the Strategic Air Command waited for the President's order.

MISCALCULATION

Even greater than the risk that Kennedy or Soviet Premier Khrushchev would deliberately start a war, was that of a war starting by accident, through miscalculation or error. On 27 October, a US plane flew off course into Soviet air space, giving the impression that an attack was under way. On the same day, in Cuba, a Soviet general decided, on his own initiative, to shoot down a US plane.

'Nuclear catastrophe was hanging by a thread,' said Soviet General Anatoly Gribkov, 'and we weren't counting days or hours, but minutes.'

▲ In 1962, Cuba was a small, weak country, caught between the rival superpowers. This British cartoon shows the island as a little boat in a violent storm, blown in different directions by Khrushchev, on the left, and Kennedy.

IN THE KREMLIN

Soviet Premier Khrushchev described the crisis in his memoirs:

'I spent one of the most dangerous nights at the Council of Ministers office in the Kremlin. I slept on a couch in my office — and I kept my clothes on… I was ready for alarming news to come at any moment, and I wanted to be ready to react immediately.'

KHRUSHCHEV REMEMBERS BY NIKITA KHRUSHCHEV

CHAPTER TWO

Cold Warriors

THE CUBAN MISSILE Crisis was just one event in the Cold War, the long confrontation between the United States and the Soviet Union, lasting from 1945 until the collapse of the Soviet system in 1991.

Although the two superpowers had been allies in World War Two, there were serious ideological differences between them. As the war drew to an end, in 1945, these differences came into the open. Each power imposed its own political system on the countries its armies occupied.

The USA was the world's leading capitalist country. Its society was based on the principle of individual liberty: the freedom of the individual to own capital, or wealth; freedom of the press; and freedom to choose the government in multi-party elections.

The Soviet system was Communist, founded on the principle of equality. Instead of individual ownership, there was collective ownership of property: all industries were run by the state. There was only one political party and a censored press. The ideal was to 'build Socialism', a society based on co-operation rather than competition.

▲ Elected at the age of 43, John F. Kennedy was the youngest US President in history. The Cuban Missile Crisis would be the hardest test of his life.

KENNEDY AND KHRUSHCHEV

Both John Kennedy and Nikita Khrushchev had strong personal reasons for believing in their own political systems. Kennedy was the son of a millionaire. His father Joe had made his money through stock market investments, and then gone into politics, serving as ambassador to Britain in the 1930s. Joe encouraged his sons to be ambitious and competitive, and used his vast fortune to fund their political careers.

Nikita Khrushchev was the son of a peasant, and could barely read until he was in his twenties. Through hard work and political skill, he rose through the ranks of the Communist Party. He had to be ruthless to become Soviet leader. But he was also an idealist, certain that Communism was the best possible political system, and that it would one day triumph all around the world.

Khrushchev never forgot his poor background. 'I went about barefoot and in rags,' he told Western diplomats. 'When you were in the nursery I was herding cows for two kopeks.' To Khrushchev, capitalist freedom was 'the freedom to exploit, the freedom to rob, the freedom to die of starvation'.

▽ Nikita Khrushchev believed that the Soviet Union could overtake the West, and show the way forward for all humankind. Addressing the Americans, he boasted, 'We will bury you!'

DIFFERENT VIEWS

In his memoirs, Khrushchev described his vision of the Communist future:

'Progress is on our side and victory will inevitably be ours... We Communists believe that Capitalism is a hell in which labouring people are condemned to slavery. We are building Socialism... Our way of life is paradise for mankind.'

KHRUSHCHEV REMEMBERS BY NIKITA KHRUSHCHEV

John Kennedy saw Communism very differently:

'The enemy is the Communist system itself – implacable, insatiable, unceasing in its drive for world domination... It is... a struggle for supremacy between two conflicting ideologies: freedom under God versus ruthless, godless tyranny.'

KENNEDY IN A SPEECH IN SEPTEMBER 1960, QUOTED IN KENNEDY V KHRUSHCHEV, THE CRISIS YEARS BY MICHAEL R BESCHLOSS

This is all that was left of a Japanese city, Nagasaki, after a single atomic bomb was dropped on it, on 9 August 1945.

THE NUCLEAR ARMS RACE

On 6 August 1945, the United States dropped the first atomic bomb on the Japanese city of Hiroshima. A single bomb now had the power to destroy a city and kill 80,000 people immediately. Three days later, when a second bomb was dropped on Nagasaki, killing a further 75,000 people, Japan surrendered. US President Harry Truman, who had ordered the bombings, declared that his new weapon was 'the greatest thing in history!'

The US had unleashed a weapon with the potential to end human civilization. Hiroshima and Nagasaki showed that it was a weapon they were prepared to use. Not surprisingly, the Soviets reacted by building their own atom bomb, which they successfully tested in September 1949.

The Americans' response was to invent an even more terrible weapon: the hydrogen, or H-bomb, which could produce an explosion a thousand times greater than an atom bomb. When it was tested, in November 1952, it destroyed an entire Pacific island. Nine months later, the Soviets also exploded an H-bomb.

MISSILES

The H-bomb was small and light. This meant that, unlike the heavy atom bomb, which had to be dropped from planes, an H-bomb could be fired as a warhead in a missile. The USA already had the world's best missile scientists. They were Germans who had developed rocket weapons for Adolf Hitler during World War Two. In the 1950s, they set about inventing missiles which could carry H-Bombs over great distances. By 1957, they had produced the Atlas, which could travel 9,700 km and land within 1.5 km of its target. It was the first **ICBM** (intercontinental ballistic missile).

DETERRENCE

H-bombs had such terrible destructive power that they could no longer be thought of as war-fighting weapons. A new strategy, or way of thinking about war, developed. The whole purpose of nuclear bombs was now to deter the enemy from beginning a war, because of the terrible consequences for their own country.

'MILITARY-INDUSTRIAL COMPLEX'

The perceived threat from the Soviet Union was one reason for the US nuclear arms build-up. Another was the fact that, to win World War Two, the USA had created a huge armaments industry, employing three and a half million men and women. After the war, this industry needed to find a new role, and one was provided by building missiles.

The US military and the arms industry formed a powerful pressure group, which US President Eisenhower called 'the military-industrial complex'.

THE ARMAMENTS INFLUENCE

In his last speech as President, in January 1961, Eisenhower warned against the influence of the 'military-industrial complex':

'This conjunction of an immense military establishment and a large arms industry is new in the American experience. The total influence – economic, political, even spiritual – is felt in every city, every State house, every office of the Federal government… In the councils of government, we must guard against the acquisition of unwarranted influence, whether sought or unsought, by the military-industrial complex.'

PUBLIC PAPERS OF THE PRESIDENTS

▼ President Harry Truman ordered the dropping of the atomic bombs, in order to end the war and save the lives of American servicemen. But he had started the nuclear arms race, which would threaten the existence of the whole planet.

KHRUSHCHEV'S BLUFF

On 4 October 1957, the Soviet Union launched a rocket carrying the first artificial space satellite, Sputnik. The launch stunned the USA, for it suggested that the Soviets were now able to build long-range missiles.

Nikita Khrushchev was happy to let the Americans think this. In late 1959, he claimed that his missiles could 'hit a fly in space'. Khrushchev said that Soviet factories were turning out ICBMs 'like sausages'.

This was a bluff. Soviet scientists could send a rocket into space, but they were unable to match the accuracy of American ICBMs. During test flights, their ICBMs often flew hundreds of kilometres off course. The Soviets could only build effective shorter range missiles, which could target western Europe, but not reach the USA.

Khrushchev did not want to spend more money on the military. His aim was to raise Soviet living standards and rebuild the economy, which had been shattered by World War Two. He welcomed nuclear weapons because they were potentially cheaper than conventional forces, but he did not want to build vast numbers of them. He hoped that nuclear bluff would be a substitute for real weapons.

THE 'MISSILE GAP'

Khrushchev's bluff convinced many Americans that there was now a 'missile gap' in the Soviet Union's favour.

US AND SOVIET STRATEGIC WARHEADS

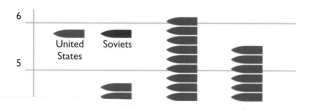

6

5

United States   Soviets

▲ In April 1962, John Kennedy looks through the periscope of a new Polaris submarine.

Even so, Kennedy went ahead with his arms build-up. By 1961, the USA possessed 18,000 nuclear weapons, with a million times the destructive power of the bomb dropped on Hiroshima. America now had a seventeen-to-one superiority in nuclear weapons.

In October 1961, Kennedy called Khrushchev's bluff by announcing to the world how far behind the Soviets really were.

'SECOND STRIKE'

US strategists always feared that the Soviet Union might consider a nuclear war winnable with a 'first strike'. Their answer was to deter a Soviet attack by developing a 'second strike' capability: the ability to survive a 'first strike' and hit back. This was the justification for building thousands of nuclear weapons.

The perfect 'second-strike' weapon was the Polaris, a submarine-launched missile, developed by the USA in 1960. Even if all the land-based missile sites in the USA were knocked out in a surprise attack, the Polaris submarine fleet would still be able to get through and devastate the Soviet Union.

CHAPTER THREE

Revolutionary Cuba

140 KM SOUTH OF Florida lies Cuba, the largest island in the Caribbean. Cuba's size, and position close to Florida, means that the USA has always had a special interest in the island.

Direct US involvement began in the 1890s, when the Cubans rose in rebellion against their Spanish rulers. In 1898, the USA entered the war on Cuba's side. They swiftly defeated the Spaniards, who were forced to give up Cuba, as well as the Philippines and Puerto Rico, which became US colonies. Although the Cubans had done most of the fighting, they were not even invited to the peace talks with Spain.

After the war, the US army occupied Cuba for four years. In 1902, the island was at last granted independence, but on US terms. Under the new constitution, the US government had the right to intervene in Cuba whenever it felt its interests

▼ This is the Texaco oil refinery at Santiago de Cuba. Texaco was just one of the US big businesses which invested heavily in Cuba.

were threatened. Cuba also had to accept the presence of a large US military base, at Guantanamo Bay.

Cuba was governed by a series of corrupt rulers. One of the worst was Fulgencio Batista, who dominated Cuba from 1933. At first, he ruled as a power behind the scenes, controlling five Cuban presidents in a row. In 1952, when it appeared that a rival might win the elections, he staged a coup and made himself dictator. By demanding bribes and protection money, he amassed a personal fortune of three hundred million dollars.

HAVANA

Under Batista, the island's capital, Havana, became a favourite destination for American tourists, who came for the gambling and nightlife. A chain of luxury hotels and casinos was built along Havana's seafront. Behind the seafront, Havana was a city of slums with around 5,000 beggars.

PEASANTS

In the countryside, the mass of the peasantry lived in poverty. Their main work, cutting sugar cane, was seasonal; for six months of the year, they might be unemployed. The peasants lived in wooden huts without running water, toilets or electricity. They had few schools and almost no doctors. It was said that Cuba was a land where only cattle were vaccinated.

▲ In the 1950s, Fulgencio Batista's open corruption and brutal treatment of political opponents, made him increasingly unpopular with the Cuban people.

US BUSINESS IN CUBA

Following independence, US businesses invested heavily in the island. By the 1950s, the United States controlled 90 per cent of Cuba's mines and cattle ranches, almost 100 per cent of the oil-refining industry, 50 per cent of the railways, and 40 per cent of the sugar industry. Almost all consumer goods in the shops were imported from the USA.

FIDEL CASTRO

In December 1956, a little group of eighty-one revolutionaries sailed from Mexico, where they had been training, to Cuba. Their leader was a thirty-one-year-old lawyer called Fidel Castro.

Castro's men found safety in the mountains of the Sierra Maestra, which became their base for a guerrilla campaign lasting three years. Castro promised to restore democracy and

▼ In 1957, Fidel Castro was photographed by a US journalist in his mountain hideout. The bearded young guerrilla leader fascinated US newspaper readers, who did not know what to make of him.

freedom, and won the backing of a broad range of Cubans. By the end of the campaign, Batista had become so unpopular that even the USA no longer supported him. On New Year's Day in 1959, he fled the country. Castro entered Havana in triumph.

Castro was left-wing, but he did not see himself as a Communist in 1959. He was a nationalist, whose main goal was to give Cubans back their independence and self-respect. He promised to end the island's reliance on the USA and to introduce sweeping social reforms.

CONFLICT WITH THE USA

One of Castro's first reforms was to break up the great landholdings, which had been mostly owned by US businesses. Castro redistributed the land among small peasant co-operatives.

The United States government reacted to this land seizure by reducing the amount of sugar it bought from Cuba. This only prompted Castro to seize more US property. President Eisenhower then banned all Cuban sugar imports. Castro warned that the US ban would 'cost Americans in Cuba down to the nails in their shoes'.

SOVIET CREDITS

Castro was desperate to find other trading partners for Cuba. He approached the Soviet Union, who agreed to buy all the sugar Cuba produced. In exchange for the sugar, Khrushchev offered Castro credits to buy Soviet machinery and oil. When the US refineries in Cuba refused to refine the Soviet oil, Castro simply nationalized them.

SOVIET TRADE

Alexander Alexeyev, a Russian journalist in Cuba, acted as messenger between Castro and Khrushchev:

'Fidel… asked if we could buy some of his sugar – at least a symbolic quantity… When I handed [Khrushchev's reply] to Fidel, it said that we, the Soviet Union, were ready to buy all the sugar, those 700,000 tons rejected by the Americans. And not only that year's consignment but also the next year's. That was really an event! I was at the rally. There were one million people there. I could see for myself the joy of the Cuban people. They were throwing their berets in the air.'

ALEXANDER ALEXEYEV QUOTED IN KENNEDY V KHRUSHCHEV, THE CRISIS YEARS BY MICHAEL R BESCHLOSS

Castro promised a
better future for the
children of Cuba.

THE NEW CUBA

After taking power, Fidel Castro introduced a series of radical
reform measures which changed life for every Cuban citizen.

A DIVIDED NATION

Castro's system divided the Cuban people. Many middle-class Cubans had initially supported him. But when he refused to allow elections or a free press, they felt that he had betrayed the revolution. The economic reforms also hit them badly. They lost the employment provided by US businesses, and their income from rents. They emigrated in their thousands to the USA, where they denounced Castro as a Communist dictator.

Yet Castro had mass support from Cuba's poor. For the first time, they were being provided with decent homes, health-care and education. Before the revolution, black and mixed-race Cubans had been second-class citizens. One of Castro's first acts was to open the white-only beaches to all Cubans. With measures such as this, and his campaign against illiteracy, Castro seemed to be breaking down the island's old barriers between classes and races. There was a new sense of solidarity and pride.

The popularity of the regime was shown by the thousands of ordinary Cubans who joined the people's militia. They were unprofessional, part-time soldiers, who kept their guns at home, and who were ready to rush to defend the revolution at Fidel's call. No hated dictator could allow so many private citizens to own weapons.

Castro was a new type of Cuban leader. Instead of making himself rich, like Batista, he lived simply. He was often photographed cutting sugar-cane alongside the workers in the fields, showing that he was a man of the people, working to improve Cubans' lives.

CHARISMA

Everyone who met Castro was struck by his charisma (ability to attract and inspire followers). Even an enemy, the US politician, Richard Nixon, remarked on this:

'Castro was one of the most striking foreign officials I met during my eight years as Vice President. He seemed to have that indefinable quality which, for good or evil, makes a leader of men. He had a compelling intense voice, sparkling black eyes, and he radiated vitality.'

FROM THE BRINK; CUBA, CASTRO AND JOHN F KENNEDY, 1964 BY DAVID DETZER

In Cuba, Alexander Alexeyev was impressed by the hero-worship Castro inspired:

'I found that at least ninety per cent of the people were for Fidel… They idolized him… Every Cuban house had graffiti saying, "Fidel, this is your home!"'

ALEXANDER ALEXEYEV QUOTED IN KENNEDY V KHRUSHCHEV, THE CRISIS YEARS BY MICHAEL R BESCHLOSS

BAY OF PIGS

In January 1961, John Fitzgerald Kennedy became President of the United States. The new President was told that plans were already in place to overthrow Fidel Castro with an invasion by an army of 1,500 Cuban émigrés. For months, the Central Intelligence Agency (CIA) had been training the émigrés in bases in Guatemala.

Allan Dulles, head of the CIA, told Kennedy that the invasion had an excellent chance of succeeding. Dulles and Kennedy both believed that Castro was deeply unpopular in Cuba. Once the invasion took place, Dulles said, there would be a general uprising against Fidel. Best of all, Kennedy could deny any involvement in the operation. The President gave his approval, on the condition that no US troops were used.

FIASCO

The invasion of Cuba, which began on 14 April 1961, was a disastrous failure. The Cuban émigrés found themselves trapped on their beach-head at the Bay of Pigs, on the south coast of Cuba, hemmed in by swamps; the CIA had chosen the worst possible place to invade. The invaders were outgunned and easily defeated by troops led personally by Castro.

As the scale of the defeat became clear, Admiral Burke of the Navy begged

THE CIA

The Central Intelligence Agency was set up in 1947 to gather international intelligence affecting US national security. The CIA later specialized in covert (secret) operations - acts which

AFTERMATH

Following the Bay of Pigs, Castro's regime was stronger than ever. He became even more hostile towards the USA and, in December 1961, declared that he was a Marxist.

The new President of the United States had been humiliated. Kennedy bitterly reproached himself for having listened to the military experts. He said, 'All my life I've known better than to depend on the experts. How could I have been so stupid, to let them go ahead?'

▲ Cuban émigrés, captured during the disastrous Bay of Pigs invasion, are marched to prison.

CALL TO ARMS

On 4 February 1962, Castro called on the poor of Latin America to stage their own revolutions:

'Now history will have to take the poor of America into account, the exploited and spurned of Latin America… And the wave of anger, of demands for justice, of claims for rights, which is beginning to sweep Latin America will not stop.'

FIDEL CASTRO SPEAKS EDITED BY MARTIN KENNER AND JAMES PETRAS

CHAPTER FOUR

Cold Warfare

A MONTH AFTER the Bay of Pigs, Kennedy travelled to Vienna in Austria, to meet the Soviet Premier. Khrushchev was in a confident mood. While Kennedy had been humiliated at the Bay of Pigs, Khrushchev had just had a great public relations triumph. On 12 April 1961, the Soviet Union sent the first man into space, the cosmonaut Yuri Gagarin.

Cuba was only briefly discussed. Khrushchev told Kennedy that the island was not a threat to the USA. He said that Castro was not even a Communist, but 'you are well on the way to making him a good one'.

BERLIN

The most important business was the question of Berlin, which seemed a much more dangerous Cold War 'hot spot' than Cuba. Although Berlin was in the heart of Communist East Germany, the Communists only controlled the eastern part of the city. West Berlin was, in Kennedy's words, 'an island of freedom in a Communist sea'. It survived thanks to its occupying force of US, French and British troops. The occupation was justified because, on paper, World War Two had not formally ended. There had been no peace treaty to settle the status of Germany.

DIVIDED GERMANY

At the end of World War Two, the Soviet Union and the USA disagreed over the future of Germany. The Americans wanted a democratic united Germany, with Berlin as its capital. The Soviets, who had lost twenty million dead at German hands, were determined to keep the country divided. In East Germany, they set up a Communist state, the German Democratic Republic (GDR), which the Americans refused to recognize. West Germany became the democratic Federal Republic.

KHRUSHCHEV'S DEMANDS

The problem for Khrushchev was that, every week, around 10,000 East Germans fled to the West, using Berlin as their escape route. They were the best educated East Germans. They knew they could earn much more money in West Germany, where there was an economic boom. Their departure threatened to ruin the East German economy.

In Vienna, Khrushchev demanded that Kennedy sign a peace treaty recognizing East Germany, and giving it control over West Berlin. If Kennedy refused, Khrushchev said that, in six months, he would sign his own peace treaty with the East Germans.

Khrushchev deliberately tried to intimidate Kennedy. He smashed the table with his hand and cried, 'I want peace. But if you want war, that is your problem.' Kennedy replied, 'It is you, not I, who wants to force a change.'

▼ Kennedy greets Khrushchev in Vienna. Once the talks began, the smiles on their faces quickly vanished.

▲ East Germans build a wall to seal the barrier between the two halves of Berlin.

THE BERLIN WALL

At midnight on 12 August 1961, without warning, the East Germans started building a barrier across Berlin, sealing off the Communist controlled eastern half from the West. The barrier was at first made of barbed wire, which was soon replaced by a concrete wall.

WALL OR WAR?

The building of the wall caused widespread alarm in West Berlin, where it was seen as a prelude to a Soviet take-

For the rest of 1961, tension between the Soviet Union and the USA over Berlin remained high. Yet Khrushchev allowed his December deadline to pass without signing the threatened treaty with the East Germans. The Berlin crisis faded from the news. Even so, for the rest of his presidency, Kennedy remained worried about Berlin. At any moment, Khrushchev could spark a new crisis and seize the city.

Building the wall solved Khrushchev's problem of East Germans fleeing west, but it was also a climbdown. Despite his explanation that the wall was built 'to guard the gates of the Socialist paradise', everyone knew that it was there to imprison the East Germans. Its existence undermined the legitimacy of the East German state.

In 1961, few people could have guessed that the Berlin Wall would stand for the next 28 years, separating families and friends. With its watchtowers, manned by guards with machine guns and dogs, it stood as a powerful symbol of Communist tyranny.

▼ In August 1961, a US tank makes a show of force on a Berlin street.

STIRRING THINGS UP

Bobby Kennedy described the aim of Operation Mongoose in a memo:

'My idea is to stir things up on the island with espionage, sabotage, general disorder, run and operated by the Cubans themselves... Do not know if we will be successful in overthrowing Castro but we have nothing to lose...'

ROBERT KENNEDY AND HIS TIMES BY ARTHUR M SCHLESINGER JNR

THE SECRET WAR

While the Berlin crisis filled the newspapers, another phase of the Cold War had begun, in secret. In November 1961, President Kennedy authorized 'Operation Mongoose', a new plan to strike at Fidel Castro.

The plan was supervised by John Kennedy's younger brother, Bobby, the attorney general (head of the Justice Department). Bobby was the President's closest adviser and the one man he trusted completely. After the Bay of Pigs, both brothers felt personally vengeful towards Castro. They were determined to overthrow him.

Bobby took the idea to the Central Intelligence Agency. The heads of the CIA were enthusiastic. They welcomed the chance to restore their reputation, which had been badly damaged by the Bay of Pigs. With a fifty million dollar budget, they set up a huge operations centre in Miami, Florida, employing 400 US and 2,000 Cuban agents. In the first seven months of 1962, the Operation Mongoose team carried out around 6,000 acts of sabotage, blowing up bridges and factories, burning fields of sugar

At the same time, the US government let it be known that, in October 1962, marines would stage large-scale exercises in the Caribbean, off Puerto Rico. They would practise invading an island to overthrow an imaginary dictator called 'Ortsac' – 'Castro' reversed.

Fidel Castro was certain that these acts were a prelude to another US invasion. He had his own agents in Florida. They reported back that there was common talk among the Cuban émigrés that there would be a new invasion. This time, people said, the Americans would get it right.

President Kennedy did not intend to invade Cuba. But everything he did convinced Castro that a real invasion was about to take place. He passed the alarming news on to the Soviet Union.

El Encanto, one of Havana's biggest department stores, lies in ruins. It had been burned down by Cuban saboteurs, trained and armed by the CIA.

CIA PLOTS

The CIA invented many schemes to kill or discredit Castro. They included:
- Sending Castro a present of a sub-aqua suit impregnated with deadly bacteria (Castro was a keen diver).
- Giving Castro a cigar soaked with the drug LSD to make him talk nonsense during one of his long speeches.
- Dosing Castro with a powder which would make his beard fall out, robbing him of his charisma.
- Distributing fake photographs showing 'an obese Castro with two beauties… ostensibly within a room in the Castro residence, lavishly furnished and a table briming [sic] over with the most delectable Cuban food with an underlying caption… such as "My ration is different."'

OPERATION MONGOOSE DOCUMENT

CHAPTER FIVE

Khrushchev's Missile Gamble

FIDEL CASTRO CONVINCED Nikita Khrushchev that the USA was about to invade Cuba. Khrushchev felt that he had to do something to protect the only Communist state in the West. Sometime in the spring of 1962, he decided that the answer was to install nuclear missiles in Cuba.

▼ Castro and Khrushchev each needed the other: Castro needed Khrushchev's weapons and trade; Khrushchev needed Castro as an example of a Communist leader who was actually popular.

STRATEGIC BALANCE

Protecting Cuba was not the only motive for sending in the missiles. The previous September, the Americans had humiliated Khrushchev by announcing that,

despite his claims, there was no 'missile gap' in the Soviet Union's favour. Khrushchev was now under great pressure from the Soviet military to increase spending on long-range and submarine-launched missiles, which could reach the USA. Yet Khrushchev wanted to cut, not increase the military budget. Military spending undermined his central political aim, which was to raise the living standards of Soviet citizens.

The Soviet Union had few long-range missiles, yet they did have short-range missiles. Placing these in Cuba, next door to the USA, seemed a cheap and easy way of cutting down the American lead.

PROTECTING CUBA

In his memoirs, Khrushchev explained why protecting Cuba was so important:

'We had an obligation to do everything in our power to protect Cuba's existence as a Socialist country and as a working example to the other countries of Latin America… One thought kept hammering at my brain: what will happen if we lose Cuba? I knew it would be a terrible blow to Marxism-Leninism. It would gravely diminish our stature throughout the world, but especially in Latin America.'

KHRUSHCHEV REMEMBERS BY NIKITA KHRUSHCHEV

PRESTIGE

Missiles in Cuba would enormously boost Soviet prestige. This was particularly important in 1962 because Khrushchev had fallen out with Mao Tse-Tung, ruler of Communist China. Mao accused Khrushchev of weakness in failing to drive the Americans out of Berlin. He challenged the Soviet Union's status as the world leader of Communism.

In his dealings with the USA, Khrushchev had often suffered from a sense of inferiority. He felt that the Americans treated his country as a second-class power. Khrushchev believed that the Soviet Union was now a superpower, and should be able to act like one. He bitterly resented the fact that the US had put missiles in Turkey, close to the Soviet border. He later wrote that, by sending missiles to Cuba, he 'would be doing nothing more than giving them a bit of their own medicine'.

Despite all the potential benefits of Cuban missiles, putting them in would be a huge gamble. Khrushchev had no idea how Kennedy would react.

▲ In October 1962, a Soviet cargo ship, loaded with missiles, steams towards Cuba.

SECRET INSTALLATION

Khrushchev believed that the only way to install missiles in Cuba was to do it secretly. If he announced his plan in advance, the Americans would be certain to react. Khrushchev might then have to back down.

Yet there were big disadvantages with secret installation. If Khrushchev had acted openly, Kennedy would have had a difficult time rallying world opinion against him. Khrushchev would only have been doing what the USA had already done in Turkey.

INTERVIEWED IN BBC TV PROGRAMME *EYEBALL TO EYEBALL* (1992)

In fact, the cargo ships were loaded with 162 nuclear warheads and missiles, and 42 jet bombers, capable of carrying nuclear weapons. There were also many conventional weapons, including 150 jet fighter planes, 350 tanks and 700 anti-aircraft guns.

The summer also saw the arrival of passenger ships, carrying 42,000 Soviet troops and technicians. The first arrivals were dressed as tourists in khaki shorts and white short-sleeved shirts. They aroused the suspicion of American observers, who noticed that they wore only two types of shirt, and that they formed in disciplined ranks on the dockside before moving out in truck convoys.

RUSSIA'S MISSILES

STRATEGIC WEAPONS
(i.e. weapons which could target cities across the USA)
SS-4s. Medium range ballistic missiles (MRBMs) fired from mobile launchers, with a range of 1,700 km.
SS-5s. Intermediate range ballistic missiles (IRBMs), with a range of 3,600 km. They had to be fired from specially built launch pads.

TACTICAL WEAPONS
(i.e. short-range weapons to be used against enemy forces in battle).
FROG-7 missiles (stands for 'free rocket over ground'). Tactical unguided missiles with a range of 40km.
Cruise missiles (slow-flying pilotless planes).

Building the missile bases was a huge operation. New roads had to be laid to take the lorries carrying the missiles. Large areas of jungle were cleared to build launch pads and storage buildings. It would be very difficult to stop the American spy planes detecting so much construction work.

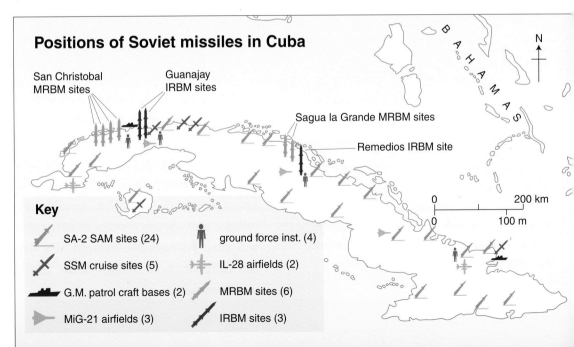

Positions of Soviet missiles in Cuba

San Christobal MRBM sites

Guanajay IRBM sites

Sagua la Grande MRBM sites

Remedios IRBM site

0 — 200 km
0 — 100 m

Key

- SA-2 SAM sites (24)
- SSM cruise sites (5)
- G.M. patrol craft bases (2)
- MiG-21 airfields (3)
- ground force inst. (4)
- IL-28 airfields (2)
- MRBM sites (6)
- IRBM sites (3)

Reacting to the Missiles

▲ A photograph of the Soviet missile sites at San Christobal, Cuba, taken by a U-2 spy plane on 25 October.

SOVIET ASSURANCES

THE AUTUMN OF 1962 was election time in the United States. Kennedy's Democratic Party was fighting the Republicans for control of Congress. The Republicans made sure that the President's handling of Cuba was a major

▼ Khrushchev had little chance of keeping his missiles secret from the U-2 planes, which made regular flights over Cuba.

PHOTOGRAPHS

On Sunday 14 October, a U-2 spy plane piloted by Major Rudolf Anderson, flew over western Cuba, taking photographs. The following day, Anderson's pictures were blown up and analysed by experts at the CIA's Photographic Interpretation Centre. The CIA experts' attention was immediately drawn to several oblong objects, which they recognized as canvas-covered missiles sitting on trailers. From their length, they could tell that these were medium range ballistic missiles, of a type known as SS-4s. With a range of 1,770 km, such missiles could strike at both New York and Washington D.C.

At 8.45 am on 16 October, McGeorge Bundy, the President's adviser on national security, broke the bad news to Kennedy, who was still in his dressing gown. Kennedy's first reaction was fury that Khrushchev had lied to him. He exclaimed, 'He can't do this to me!'

Kennedy was baffled by the discovery. He could not understand Khrushchev's motivation. Khrushchev had never placed any nuclear weapons outside the Soviet Union. Why would he now be willing to risk a war over Cuba?

Mutual misunderstanding and incomprehension would be a major problem throughout the coming crisis.

THE U-2

The U-2, designed in 1955, was a spy plane which could fly at altitudes of 21km. It took off almost vertically, and flew at 740 km an hour. Its purpose was to take photographs unobserved and out of the reach of anti-aircraft guns. On its belly it carried seven cameras with amazingly sophisticated lenses. In 1955, the Air Force published pictures of a golf course taken by a U-2 from a height of 15,000 m. The pictures clearly showed golf balls lying on the grass.

31

IN THE WHITE HOUSE

At 11.45 am on 16 October, the President assembled his chief advisers in the White House to discuss the missile crisis. For the next twelve days, the advisers met continuously. The group would later be known as Ex-Comm, which is short for 'Executive Committee of the National Security Council'.

Kennedy blamed the Bay of Pigs disaster on his failure to listen to a wide enough range of advice. Now he encouraged completely open discussion, with all opinions given equal weight. To encourage frankness, the President decided not to attend all the meetings. He sensed that people often told him what they thought he wanted to hear.

The advisers met in secret for the first five days of the crisis, pretending to the outside world that nothing was wrong. On 18 October, Kennedy saw Andrei Gromyko, the Soviet Foreign Minister. When Gromyko repeated Khrushchev's assurance that he would never send offensive weapons to Cuba, Kennedy had to hide his anger.

EX-COMM

There were twenty members of Ex-Comm, though eight only attended occasional meetings. The most important members were:

Robert McNamara, Secretary of Defence
Paul Nitze, Assistant Secretary of Defence
Dean Rusk, Secretary of State
George Ball, Under Secretary of State

The one thing that the Ex-Comm members agreed on was that the President had to act to remove the missiles. Kennedy could not allow Castro's Cuba to threaten the USA with nuclear weapons. If he failed to act, he could be impeached: tried for misconduct and thrown out of office.

But all Ex-Comm could do was offer advice. The final decision and responsibility rested with the President alone. Gazing out of the window, President Kennedy said ruefully, 'I guess I'd better earn my salary this week.'

▲ The President meets Soviet Foreign Minister, Gromyko, and Ambassador Dobrynin. On the surface, the meeting seemed friendly. But Kennedy, who now knew about the missiles, was secretly furious.

PRESSURE

Bobby Kennedy described the awesome sense of responsibility that the members of Ex-Comm felt:

'Each one of us was being asked to make a recommendation which, if wrong and if accepted, could mean the destruction of the human race.'

13 DAYS BY ROBERT F KENNEDY

HOW DO WE STOP?

The leading opponent of a surprise attack was the Secretary of Defence, Robert McNamara, who said:

'I don't know quite what kind of a world we live in after we've struck Cuba, and we, we've started it... How, how do we stop at that point?'

THE KENNEDY TAPES: INSIDE THE WHITE HOUSE DURING THE CUBAN MISSILE CRISIS EDITED BY E R MAY AND P D ZELIKOW

OPTIONS

While Ex-Comm was arguing about the President's options in the White House, the Joint Chiefs of Staff (military bosses) had their own meetings in the Pentagon. Their attitude was summed up by Air Force Chief General Curtis LeMay. His solution was simple: 'Bomb the hell out of them!'

To avoid the risk of retaliation, the chiefs favoured a large scale surprise strike on the missile sites. General Maxwell Taylor pointed out that if the Soviets received any warning, they could hide the missiles in the Cuban jungles. Then the military would never be able to get them out.

The President asked the chiefs what they thought the Soviets would do when he attacked Cuba. General LeMay assured him that they would do nothing. Kennedy was sceptical. He said, 'If they don't take action in Cuba, they certainly will in Berlin.'

DOUBTS

As the debate continued, the members of Ex-Comm felt growing doubts about a surprise attack. It was strongly argued against by Bobby Kennedy and Robert

McNamara. They remembered World War Two, and the outrage that all Americans felt when Pearl Harbor was attacked by the Japanese in a surprise raid. Japanese General Tojo had been hanged as a war criminal for that attack. How could the USA now adopt the same tactic?

THE BLOCKADE OPTION

McNamara suggested an alternative tactic. The USA should impose a naval blockade. This would mean stopping and searching all Soviet ships heading for Cuba, and turning back any carrying weapons. The advantage of a blockade was that it was a limited form of pressure, which would give Khrushchev a chance to back down. If the blockade failed, pressure on Khrushchev could be increased in other ways. The USA might still have to attack Cuba, but only if the blockade did not work.

THE MORAL POSITION

Bobby Kennedy described his reasons for opposing the surprise attack:

'Like others, I could not accept the idea that the United States would rain bombs on Cuba, killing thousands and thousands of civilians in a surprise attack… They were… advocating a surprise attack by a very large nation against a very small one. This, I said, could not be undertaken if we were to maintain our moral position at home and around the globe. Our struggle against Communism throughout the world was far more than physical survival.'

13 Days by Robert F Kennedy

▼ Secretary of Defence, Robert McNamara, speaks to the press in August 1961, at the height of the Berlin crisis.

THE MILITARY VIEW

General Taylor explains why he was strongly against the blockade:

'*Khrushchev could simply bring his ships just short of the quarantine line and stand there and scream to the world over the violation of international law we were indulging in, and meanwhile start that argument going while his missiles completed their readiness in the island.*'

ON THE BRINK: AMERICANS AND SOVIETS RE-EXAMINE THE CUBAN MISSILE CRISIS BY JAMES G BLIGHT AND DAVID WELCH

THE PRESIDENT DECIDES

On Saturday afternoon, 20 October, John Kennedy announced his decision to Ex-Comm. He would impose a naval blockade on Cuba before he launched an air strike.

General Taylor argued forcefully against the decision. He said that a blockade would not get the weapons out that were already there. Military force would eventually have to be used. All Kennedy would be doing was giving the Soviets time to get their missiles ready. He would also be inviting the Soviets to impose their own blockade on Berlin.

A blockade was also illegal. Under international law, no country was allowed to stop the ships of another in international waters. To get around the legal problem, Kennedy decided to call the blockade a 'quarantine'.

▼ The President tells the nation about the missile crisis, in a television broadcast from the White House.

Kennedy refused to change his decision, which was supported by the majority of Ex-Comm. Later, at a meeting with the chiefs, General Sweeney admitted to Kennedy that even a surprise attack could not be certain of destroying all the missile sites. This convinced the President that the blockade was the only justifiable option.

GETTING READY

Now the decision had been made, the machinery of government went into action. Over the weekend, the navy sent 180 ships to the Caribbean, while troops were moved to the southern states of the USA. Around the world, US armed forces were put on alert in case of Soviet attack.

At the same time, the leaders of NATO countries and the Organization of American States were told about the missiles. They all offered to support the President.

TELLING THE PUBLIC

On Monday evening, 22 October, Kennedy made a television broadcast from the White House. Millions of Americans watched the programme, while the talk was also broadcast on radio across Europe.

The President told a shocked public that the Soviets were building offensive missile sites on the 'imprisoned island' of Cuba. He stressed the fact that Khrushchev had lied repeatedly, assuring him that missiles would never be installed there. Kennedy then explained his decision to impose a quarantine.

'The cost of freedom is always high,' said the President, 'but Americans have always paid it. And one path we shall never choose, and that is the path of surrender or submission.'

▲ A US naval destroyer, the Lawrence, sets off from its base in Puerto Rico to take part in the blockade of Cuba.

FRENCH SUPPORT

When French President De Gaulle was shown the photographs of the missile bases, he said:

'Tell President Kennedy, he must do what he has to do. And if this leads to World War Three, France will be with the United States.'

AS I SAW IT BY DEAN RUSK

Anti-war protesters
took to the streets all
over the world.

WORLD REACTIONS

Around the world, people were stunned by Kennedy's speech. Although western heads of state all backed the President, the reactions of private citizens varied greatly.

There was already widespread unease about nuclear weapons. This feeling was captured in *On the Beach*, a popular

At the same time, other groups called for even stronger action by Kennedy. There was an anti-Castro rally in Madison Square Garden, New York, where 8,000 people chanted 'Fight! Fight! Fight!'

Opinion polls showed that most US citizens backed the President. The newspapers had already warned the public about the Soviet military build-up in Cuba. Many felt that Kennedy's action was long overdue. Questioned by pollsters, people said, 'We've been pushed around long enough'.

Outside the USA, Kennedy's blockade had much less support. Across Latin America, there were anti-US riots. In London, thousands of demonstrators marched on the US embassy, shouting 'Viva Fidel! Kennedy to hell!'

The British press accused Kennedy of overreacting to the Cuban missiles. For years, the British and other European countries had lived with Soviet missiles aimed at them. Why couldn't the Americans learn to live with the same danger?

ACROSS THE USA

A Los Angeles grocer, Sam Goldstad, told a journalist about the panic buying he witnessed in his shop:

'They're nuts. One lady's working four shopping carts at once. Another lady bought twelve packages of detergents. What's she going to do, wash up after the bomb?'

The only people who were pleased by Kennedy's speech were the Cuban émigrés. Sanchez Arango, an émigré leader, spoke on Miami television:

'This is the beginning of the end for Castro. We are very happy. The President is a wonderful man.'

THE BRINK: CUBA, CASTRO AND JOHN F KENNEDY BY DAVID DETZER

IN THE SOVIET UNION

Nikita Khrushchev was shocked by Kennedy's speech. His 'missile gamble' had backfired in the worst possible way. According to Anatoly Dobrynin, Soviet ambassador to the USA, Khrushchev 'had no fallback plan to deal with such a reverse' and was in a state of 'total bewilderment'.

On Tuesday afternoon, Radio Moscow broadcast news of the crisis. The US blockade was presented as an act of unjustified aggression. No mention was made of any Soviet missiles in Cuba.

To keep people calm, Khrushchev and the entire Soviet leadership went to an opera at the Bolshoi Theatre. However, everyone knew that such an unusual event was a sure sign that a major crisis was under way.

CHAPTER SEVEN

The Blockade

FIDEL CASTRO WAS aware of all the US activity over the weekend. He later recalled that he 'understood by instinct, by smell, that something would happen'. Even before he heard Kennedy's speech on 22 October, he began to call out the Cuban militia.

For the Cubans, the crisis did not begin with Kennedy's speech. It had started eighteen months earlier, with the Bay of Pigs invasion. They saw the Bay of Pigs as the beginning of an undeclared war waged against them by the USA. Since November 1961, they had been victims of the sabotage campaign of Bobby Kennedy's Operation Mongoose teams.

▼ On the Havana seafront, Cuban militiamen watch and wait for US planes. They are armed with anti-aircraft guns.

READY TO DIE

General Sergio Del Valle, chief of staff of the Cuban army, remembers the attitude of the Soviet troops in Cuba:

'Our Soviet comrades at that stage were ready to fulfil the missions with us, to die alongside us, and they expressed this several times during our visits. It is absolutely certain that our Soviet brothers would die there with us.'

BACK TO THE BRINK: PROCEEDINGS OF THE MOSCOW CONFERENCE ON THE CUBAN MISSILE CRISIS EDITED BY B J ALLEN, J G BLIGHT AND D A WELCH

The Soviets had little choice in this matter, as their General Gribkov explained:

'We had no way of leaving Cuba, no avenue for withdrawal.'

WE NOW KNOW: RETHINKING COLD WAR HISTORY BY JOHN LEWIS GADDIS

◄ The US base at Guantanamo Bay was reinforced with troops. Here the anxious marines are briefed by their commander, General Collins. These US troops in Cuba could expect to be attacked at any moment.

The Cubans had been expecting an invasion for months. Now it seemed certain to come. Kennedy's naval blockade was seen as the declaration of open war. Off the coast of Cuba, people could see the gathering US war fleet, and every day low-flying US reconnaissance planes flew overhead.

MOBILIZATION

The whole country was placed on a war footing, with 270,000 Cubans being mobilized. In Havana, major buildings were defended with barbed wire and sandbags. Anti-aircraft guns were set up in the squares, while tanks took to the streets.

Although Castro did not openly admit that he had nuclear missiles, he told the Cuban people that they now had the ability to destroy any aggressor. As a result, there was an atmosphere of defiance. Castro said that the Cubans and their Soviet allies would fight to the last man.

KHRUSHCHEV AND CASTRO

There were daily communications between Castro and Khrushchev. Castro urged the Soviet leader to keep firm and not bow down to the US demands. He said that the Cubans were ready for the coming battle.

The last thing Khrushchev had wanted was to risk starting a war over Cuba. Now one of his greatest problems would be to hold Castro back.

CASTRO'S SUGGESTION

Khrushchev was alarmed by Castro's warlike attitude, which he recalled later:

'Castro suggested that to prevent our nuclear missiles from being destroyed, we should launch a pre-emptive strike against the US. My comrades in the leadership and I realized that our friend Fidel totally failed to understand our purpose.'

THE CUBAN MISSILE CRISIS REVISITED
EDITED BY JAMES NATHAN

'EYEBALL TO EYEBALL'

On the morning of Wednesday, 24 October, two Soviet ships were approaching the quarantine line, accompanied by a Soviet submarine, which had taken up position in between them. The US Navy had orders to intercept the ships, using depth charges to force the submarine to surface. If the ships refused to stop, the Navy had orders to open fire on them.

At 10.25 am Kennedy was told that the Soviet ships had 'stopped dead in the water'. Khrushchev had made his first concession, ordering them not to cross the line. Dean Rusk, remembering the children's staring game, said, 'We're eyeball to eyeball and I think the other fellow just blinked.'

▼ Military positions for the US blockade of Cuba.

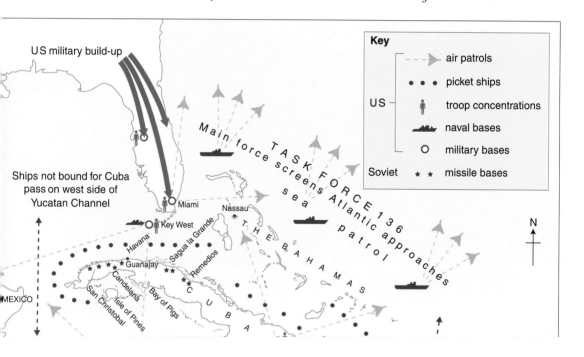

Despite Khrushchev's 'blink', the crisis was far from over. Aerial photographs demonstrated that work on the missile sites had speeded up, and was now going on day and night. For the first time, the photos also showed Soviet jet bombers being assembled.

LETTERS

As the crisis continued, Kennedy and Khrushchev exchanged a series of letters, which were sent by cable in code and then had to be decoded and translated. Khrushchev's first letters were angry and defensive, accusing the US of piracy in its illegal blockade.

On the evening of 26 October, a very different type of letter arrived from Khrushchev. At great length, he talked of the horrors of war, which he had seen at first hand. He told Kennedy that the pair of them should not 'pull on the ends of the rope in which you have tied the knots of war, because the more the two of us pull, the tighter the knot will be tied'.

Khrushchev said he would not send arms to Cuba if the President promised not to invade the island. Although he made no mention of the missiles already in place, his letter seemed to hold out hope of a solution to the crisis. For the first time, the President felt cautious optimism that war could be avoided.

ROOM TO MOVE

Kennedy was determined not to force Khrushchev into a corner, where he had to fight or be humiliated. He said to Bobby:

'If anybody is around to write after this, they are going to understand that we made every effort to find peace and every effort to give our adversary room to move. I am not going to push the Russians an inch beyond what is necessary.'

13 DAYS BY ROBERT F KENNEDY

BLACK SATURDAY

Despite the President's optimism, the following day, Saturday 27 October, proved to be the worst of the whole crisis. It came to be called 'Black Saturday'.

The first bad news arrived at 10.17 am. A second, very different message from Khrushchev was broadcast over Radio Moscow. Kennedy took this to mean that, unlike the previous message, this one was aimed at world opinion. It was much more formal than the private letter. Khrushchev now demanded the withdrawal of the US missiles in Turkey in exchange for his 'weapons' in Cuba.

The difference between Khrushchev's two offers confused all the members of Ex-Comm. What was he doing? Did it mean that hard-liners had taken over in the Kremlin?

This offer placed Kennedy in a terrible dilemma. He had already

◀ Rudolf Anderson, shot down by a Soviet missile, would be the only fatality of the Cuban crisis. His body, returned to the USA by Castro, was given a hero's burial. His wrecked plane ended up on display in a Cuban museum.

decided to get rid of the Turkish missiles; they were now seen as obsolete, and were to be replaced by Polaris submarines. But if he agreed to Khrushchev's proposal, he would be seen to be trading Turkish for US security. This would be a blow to the whole NATO alliance.

As usual, the Joint Chiefs of Staff had a simple reaction to Khrushchev's offers. They believed that he was playing for time while the missiles became operational. They drafted a formal recommendation that the President order a massive air strike for the next day, followed by a full invasion of Cuba.

THE FIRST SHOTS

Even more alarming events followed in the afternoon. Pilots returning from low-level reconnaissance flights said that the Cubans had tried to shoot them down. Then Major Rudolf Anderson, the pilot who had first photographed the bases, was brought down by a missile while flying his U-2. General Taylor broke the news, 'The wreckage is on the ground and the pilot's dead.'

Kennedy knew that the missiles in Cuba were under Soviet control. This could only mean that Khrushchev had chosen to escalate the crisis, or that Soviet 'hawks' had indeed taken over.

The news created a sense of urgency in the White House. The military felt they had been proved right, and urged the military strike.

A TIGHTENING NOOSE

Bobby Kennedy remembered the atmosphere, as one piece of bad news followed another:

'There was the feeling that the noose was tightening on all of us, on Americans, on mankind, and all the bridges to escape were crumbling… There was almost unanimous agreement that we had to attack early the next morning…'

13 Days by Robert F Kennedy

A LAST CHANCE

Despite the belief that war was now almost inevitable, President Kennedy decided to give Khrushchev one last chance for a peaceful solution. 'We won't attack tomorrow,' he said, 'we shall try again.'

Bobby Kennedy and Ted Sorenson, the President's speech writer, came up with a tactic. They said that the President should ignore Khrushchev's second message, demanding the Turkish trade, and reply accepting the 'offer' made in the first. They drafted a letter for Kennedy in which he pledged not to invade Cuba if Khrushchev removed his missiles. Once the Soviets had done this, the letter said, Kennedy would be willing to talk about 'other armaments'.

To impress Khrushchev with the urgency of the situation, the President asked Bobby to visit the Soviet ambassador, Anatoly Dobrynin. He told him to say that the Turkish missiles would be withdrawn eventually, but that there could be no public deal or announcement on the matter.

▲ The President's speech writer, Ted Sorenson, with his wife Sara. After Bobby Kennedy Sorensen was

Bobby was a good choice for a messenger. While John

Ambassador Dobrynin shares a joke with President Kennedy at their first meeting. His later talk with Bobby would be decisive in ending the crisis.

In his autobiography, Anatoly Dobrynin described Bobby's manner during the meeting:

'He remarked almost in passing that a lot of unreasonable people among American generals – and not only generals – were "spoiling for a fight"… Throughout the whole meeting he was very nervous; indeed it was the first time I saw him in such a state.'

Bobby described his feelings after the meeting:

'I returned to the White House. The President was not optimistic, nor was I… What hope there was now rested with Khrushchev's revising his course within the next few hours. It was a hope, not an expectation. The expectation was a military confrontation by Tuesday and possibly tomorrow.'

BOBBY'S TACTICS

Bobby had hinted that the President might lose control of the US military. According to Ex-Comm member, Douglas Dillon, this was a deliberate tactic:

'It was a brilliant way to handle it. I think he did a hell of a job convincing the Russians that the roof was going to fall in on the President. That's what he was supposed to do, and he did it.'

ON THE BRINK: AMERICANS AND SOVIETS RE-EXAMINE THE CUBAN MISSILE CRISIS
BY JAMES G BLIGHT AND DAVID WELCH

THE VIEW FROM THE KREMLIN

With each day of the crisis, Nikita Khrushchev became more desperate to find a solution. By offering to exchange Cuban for Turkish missiles, on 'Black Saturday', he had not meant to place Kennedy in a difficult position. He was searching for a solution which would allow him to back down with dignity. His reason for using a public broadcast was not to embarrass Kennedy, but to avoid the delay of a coded letter.

Anatoly Dobrynin explained the difference between Khrushchev's two messages:

'At first he had been afraid to complicate the urgent search for settlement by insisting on the removal of American missiles from Turkey. But on second thought, under pressure from some of his colleagues, he made a desperate, last-minute attempt to obtain a deal to swap his missiles in Cuba for the American missiles.'

The Turkish offer was another miscalculation. The broadcast confused Kennedy, and infuriated both the Cubans and the Turks, who resented being treated as 'bargaining chips'.

▼ Fidel Castro was utterly fearless and ready for war with the USA. Castro's warlike attitude convinced Khrushchev that he had to end the missile crisis.

LOSING CONTROL

Khrushchev was just as horrified as Kennedy by the events of 'Black Saturday'. He had given no orders for any US planes to be fired on. The orders came from Fidel Castro, who had convinced himself that a US invasion was already under way.

Major Anderson's U-2 was shot down by a Soviet general unsure of whose orders to follow. He was thousands of miles from home, surrounded by hostile US forces, which he believed Fidel Castro had already started firing on. Even though the US had not begun to invade, Castro's wild actions made an attack increasingly likely. In a moment of panic, the general gave the order to fire.

Khrushchev felt that he was losing control of events in Cuba. The shooting down of the U-2 showed him that he could not even control his own troops. He knew that now the first shots had been fired, the conflict was likely to escalate quickly.

The Soviet leader was already close to panic when he heard from Dobrynin about his talk with Bobby Kennedy. Dobrynin gave Khrushchev the impression that there was a real risk that the US military might overthrow Kennedy and launch a war. It was urgent that he end the crisis at once.

Khrushchev immediately agreed to remove the missiles. He was so anxious to end the crisis swiftly that he announced his agreement over Radio Moscow. He made no mention of the US missiles in Turkey.

KHRUSHCHEV'S SPEECH

Dobrynin criticized Khrushchev's radio broadcast:

'He was so confused that he did not play the one good card in his hand – Kennedy's agreement to withdraw US missiles from Turkey. This could have been presented to the public as a deal trading their bases for ours… Soviet citizens were stunned by the broadcast, for they had heard nothing official during the entire week about our missiles in Cuba.'

IN CONFIDENCE BY ANATOLY DOBRYNIN

▼ This US cartoon shows a terrified Khrushchev backing down, while Kennedy holds firm.

'I've Changed My Mind, Let's Argue on the Bench'

CHAPTER EIGHT

A Peaceful Solution?

▲ Khrushchev welcomes United Nations Secretary General U Thant to Moscow for the signing of the treaty to ban nuclear tests, in August 1963.

PRESIDENT KENNEDY WAS careful not to claim that the agreement with Khrushchev was a victory for the USA. He knew that Khrushchev had been placed in a difficult position, and he did not want to make it any worse for him.

Yet Kennedy could not stop the western press from presenting the agreement as his own personal triumph. Previously, he had seemed a weak Cold War leader. He had been accused of lacking guts during the Bay of Pigs, and then of failing to do anything to stop the building of the Berlin Wall. But now he had proved himself by standing up to Khrushchev, and forcing the 'Soviet bully' to back down. Nobody was told about his agreement to withdraw the missiles from Turkey.

The President was also praised for his brilliant 'crisis management'. He had kept his head throughout the thirteen days, and refused to give in to the pressure from the military to launch an invasion. The successful outcome of the crisis showed that Kennedy had made the right decisions.

WE ARE ALL MORTAL

On the day the Test Ban Treaty was agreed, Kennedy spoke to an audience of students at the American University Washington:

'WE'VE BEEN HAD!'

Only two groups of people in the USA did not see the resolution as a victory

▲ Kennedy smiles at the Dallas crowd, just moments before he is shot in the head and killed.

throughout the crisis. He was amazed at their attitude. Admiral Anderson said, 'We've been had!' General Curtis LeMay thumped the table and said, 'It is the greatest defeat in our history, Mr President...We should invade today!'

The next day, Kennedy said, 'The military are mad.'

WORKING FOR PEACE

The crisis showed that neither the USA nor the Soviet Union wanted nuclear war. Its resolution greatly strengthened Kennedy's authority as a President. He decided to use his new position of strength to work towards better relations with Khrushchev, and to reduce the nuclear threat. The result was a treaty banning nuclear tests, which Khrushchev agreed to sign on 25 July 1963.

Just four months later, Kennedy was dead, killed in Dallas by an assassin's bullet.

Chairman Mao (left) of China looked down on Khrushchev as a weak and unworthy successor to the ruthless Stalin, whom he had hero-worshipped.

KHRUSHCHEV'S HUMILIATION

On 'Black Saturday', Khrushchev had publicly called for the USA to withdraw its missiles from Turkey. Yet the following day, in the second radio broadcast, he had offered to remove his own missiles from Cuba without even mentioning those in Turkey.

Khrushchev claimed that he had secured the safety of Socialist Cuba. But every Soviet citizen could see that his failure to get concessions over the Turkish missiles was a humiliating public defeat. He had brought the world to the brink of nuclear war and gained almost nothing for it.

Khrushchev knew that he had been

A PERSONAL TRIUMPH

Khrushchev's words, the Chinese radio 'started hooting and shouting about how Khrushchev had turned coward and backed down'. They broadcast the charge that he was not fit to be world Communist leader.

Until the missile crisis, Khrushchev had managed to restrain the Chinese from building their own nuclear bombs. But now Chairman Mao said that Communist countries could no longer rely on the Soviet Union to defend them. Mao wanted China to have nuclear weapons too.

The Chinese exploded their first nuclear bomb on 16 October 1964. Just two days earlier, Nikita Khrushchev had fallen from power.

KHRUSHCHEV'S FALL

Khrushchev's position as Soviet leader was damaged by the crisis. Although his personal authority was still too great for him to be challenged in 1962, his colleagues began to lose patience with his reckless style of leadership.

When they eventually conspired against him, two years later, the first charge they levelled against Khrushchev was of 'hasty and ill-considered decisions'. They replaced him with Leonid Brezhnev, who would be the most cautious and unadventurous of all the Soviet leaders.

Leonid Brezhnev spent a year gathering support for a plot against Khrushchev, finally overthrowing him in October 1964.

A PAWN

In January 1963, Castro told a French journalist:

'Cuba does not want to be a pawn on the world's chessboard… I cannot agree with Khrushchev promising Kennedy to return the missiles without making the least reference to the indispensable approval of the Cuban government.'

KENNEDY V KHRUSHCHEV, THE CRISIS YEARS
BY MICHAEL R BESCHLOSS

CUBA BETRAYED

Fidel Castro heard about the agreement between Khrushchev and Kennedy on the radio. The Soviet leader had not even consulted him about the negotiations. Castro was so furious that he kicked a wall and smashed a mirror. He said that, if he could, he would have beaten Khrushchev to within an inch of his life.

Castro had devoted his life to Cuba's struggle for independence and dignity. He

In 1965 7 Ernesto 'Che'

had freed his homeland from the dominance of one foreign power, the USA. Now the Soviets were acting as if Cuba belonged to them. He was particularly angry at Khrushchev's agreement that United Nations inspectors could visit Cuba, to verify that the missiles had been withdrawn.

CASTRO'S DEMANDS

Castro made his own demands before he would agree to the UN inspection. He called for the US to end its campaign of sabotage against Cuba; to close down the Cuban émigrés' training camps in Puerto Rico and the USA; and to surrender their naval base in Guantanamo Bay. If the UN inspected the training camps, then they could come to Cuba. Otherwise, he warned, 'Whoever comes to inspect Cuba must come armed for battle!'

Although the missiles were removed, Castro's attitude allowed Kennedy to withhold his pledge not to invade Cuba. The CIA's secret war continued, with more Cuban factories bombed, and more assassination attempts on Castro. A new economic blockade was imposed on Cuba, which is still in force today, forty years later.

Castro summed up the crisis with these words: 'War was avoided, but peace was not gained.'

SPREADING COMMUNISM

Castro felt that he could not depend on the Soviet Union to defend Cuba. To find

CHE GUEVARA

Ernesto 'Che' Guevara, the leading figure in Castro's international guerrilla campaigns, described the scope of the struggle against 'Yankee imperialism':

'US imperialism is guilty of aggression – its crimes are enormous and cover the whole world… It must be defeated in a world confrontation… To die under the flag of Vietnam, of Venezuela, of Guatemala, of Laos, of Guinea, of Colombia, of Bolivia, of Brazil – to name only a few scenes of today's armed struggle – would be equally glorious and desirable for an American, an Asian, an African, even a European.'

VENCEREMOS! THE SPEECHES AND WRITINGS OF CHE GUEVARA
EDITED BY JOHN GERASSI

new allies and widen the struggle against the USA, he stepped up his efforts to spread Communism to Latin America and other parts of the Third World.

SECRET TALKS

While Kennedy remained publicly hostile to Castro, in private he tried a new approach. Recently published documents reveal that, in the last months of his life, he began secret talks with Castro, to try to find a way in which the USA could normalize relations with Cuba. Kennedy hoped to take advantage of Castro's anger at Khrushchev, and entice him away from his Soviet alliance. Castro welcomed the approach, but it was cut short by the President's early death.

CHAPTER NINE

Lessons of the Crisis

THE CUBAN CRISIS ended the Cold War's second phase, which had been characterized by dramatic crises. The leadership on each side now tried to avoid direct confrontations.

Both Kennedy and Khrushchev were shocked at how close they had come to nuclear war. One of their first acts after the crisis was to install a telephone link, called 'the hot-line', between the Kremlin and the White House. By communicating directly, the leaders hoped to avoid the misunderstandings which might lead to future war.

▼ American soldiers in action during the Vietnam War.

VIETNAM

Khrushchev's climb-down gave the US government increased confidence, and a willingness to take on a wider global military role. In 1965, Kennedy's successor, Lyndon Johnson, launched a massive bombing campaign against Communist North Vietnam. Soon, 50,000 US troops were also fighting in Vietnam. Lasting until 1973, the Vietnam conflict would be the longest war ever fought by the USA.

PEACE MOVEMENTS

Many people in the West felt that the successful outcome of the crisis showed the wisdom of having nuclear weapons. It was said that it was the nuclear threat that made both Khrushchev and Kennedy draw back from war. Nuclear deterrence seemed to keep the peace.

This was a blow to anti-nuclear groups, such as the British Campaign for Nuclear Disarmament. From 1958, there had been annual marches by thousands of anti-nuclear demonstrators, who walked from London to the weapons research centre at Aldermaston. The last big Aldermaston march was held in 1963.

Throughout the West, the 1960s would be a decade of anti-war protest. Millions of demonstrators, mostly young people, took to the streets of Europe and the USA. But they demonstrated not against nuclear weapons, but against the long and bloody conventional war fought by the USA in Vietnam.

KHRUSHCHEV ON KENNEDY

In retirement, Khrushchev gave his assessment of Kennedy:

'His death was a great loss. He was gifted with the ability to resolve international conflicts by negotiation, as the whole world learned during the so-called Cuban crisis. Regardless of his youth, he was a real statesman. I believe that if Kennedy had lived, relations between the Soviet Union and the United States would be much better than they are. Why do I say that? Because Kennedy would have never let his country get bogged down in Vietnam.'

KHRUSHCHEV REMEMBERS BY NIKITA KHRUSHCHEV

CONTINUING COLD WAR

The Missile Crisis had dramatically exposed Soviet weakness. When it was over, Soviet Deputy Foreign Minister V.V. Kuznetsov said, 'Never will we be caught like this again.'

In his last two years of power, Khrushchev was forced to give in to pressure from the military to increase spending on nuclear weapons. This was a bitter blow. Khrushchev had dreamed of improving the living standards of the Soviet public. Now submarines and missiles would be the priority, as the Soviet Union caught up with the USA in the arms race.

STAGNATION

Under Leonid Brezhnev, the Soviet Union became a true military superpower, with as massive a nuclear arsenal as the USA's. Yet the price was economic inefficiency, bad housing, food shortages, and a discontented population.

Khrushchev had been an idealist, who wanted to build a Communist paradise on earth. Brezhnev was a cynic, who did not even believe in Communism. He said to his brother, 'All that stuff about Communism is a tall tale for popular consumption.'

▼ In the 1990s, the loss of Soviet oil imports forced Cuba to open up its own oil fields. Between 1991 and 2000, Cuban oil production increased from 8,630 barrels a day to 44,800.

In the Soviet Union, the Brezhnev period, from 1964 until 1982, would later be known as 'the era of stagnation'. The government's failure to win public support would be a major factor in the eventual collapse of the Soviet system in 1989-91.

CASTRO TODAY

As the Soviet Union crumbled, in 1991, the Russians announced that they were withdrawing their 11,000 military advisers and technicians from Cuba. At the same time, Cuban trade with the Eastern bloc countries disappeared.

The loss of Soviet subsidies was a disaster for Castro. In 1993, he announced that Cubans would be able to own US dollars. Two years later, he allowed foreign companies to own Cuban property and open businesses. Old class differences re-emerged, as people with dollars now had access to better goods.

Despite Castro's concessions to capitalism, the US government remained as hostile as ever to him, tightening its economic blockade. To stop foreign companies investing in Cuba, in 1996, President Clinton signed the 'Helms-Burton Bill'. This gave US companies the right to sue any businesses making use of their confiscated property in Cuba.

Despite four decades of opposition from the world's most powerful nation, Fidel Castro has survived, becoming the world's longest serving political leader. At the start of the 21st century, Castro's Cuba is the last country still fighting the Cold War with the USA.

▲ Fidel Castro lived to see the worldwide collapse of Communism, but still held on to power, and to his faith in his political system.

WAITING FOR THE TRAIN TO MOVE

A Russian joke compared the different approaches of three Soviet leaders:

'Stalin, Khrushchev and Brezhnev were sitting on a train in a station, getting increasingly worried that it refused to move.

Stalin said, "Let's shoot one of the drivers. That would scare the others and make them start the train."

"That would be wrong," said Khrushchev, "We must raise the drivers' salaries and encourage them to get the train moving."

Brezhnev said, "Why don't we just close the curtains, and pretend that the train is moving?"'

Timeline

1952

1 NOVEMBER
USA explodes H-bombs on
Elugelab Island in the Pacific

1953

5 MARCH
Death of Stalin

1957

JULY
Khrushchev defeats his rivals to
become Soviet head of state

4 OCTOBER
Soviets launch Sputnik,
a space satellite

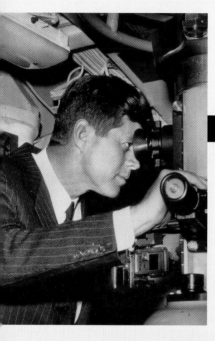

1961

20 JANUARY
John F Kennedy takes office as
President of the USA

12 APRIL
Soviet cosmonaut, Yuri Gagarin,
makes first manned space flight

14-19 APRIL
Invading army of US-backed
Cuban émigrés defeated at the
Bay of Pigs

3 JUNE
Kennedy and Khrushchev meet
in Vienna

12 AUGUST
Communists build Berlin Wall

NOVEMBER
Kennedy approves Operation
Mongoose, the secret war
against Castro

28 OCTOBER

66708

1959

1 JANUARY
Fidel Castro comes to
power in Cuba

17 MAY
Castro begins to seize
US-owned lands

1960

13 FEBRUARY
Castro signs a trade agreement
with the USSR

1962

15 OCTOBER
Spy photographs reveal the
presence of Soviet missile sites
in Cuba

22 OCTOBER
Kennedy announces the
imposition of a 'quarantine'
on Cuba

24 OCTOBER
Soviet ships turn back from the
quarantine line

27 OCTOBER
('Black Saturday')
Khrushchev demands that the US
withdraw its missiles from Turkey
A US spy plane is shot down
over Cuba

1963

25 JULY
Kennedy and Khrushchev agree
to a Nuclear Test Ban Treaty

22 NOVEMBER
Kennedy assassinated in Dallas,
Texas, by Lee Harvey Oswald

1964

14 OCTOBER
Khrushchev falls from power

16 OCTOBER
China explodes a nuclear bomb

Glossary

Ballistic missile A missile which, after its rocket motor has burned out, uses the force of gravity to reach its target.

Blockade Isolating a place by blocking all approaches to it. A blockade usually only takes place in time of war.

Capitalism Economic system based on free enterprise and the right to own individual property.

CIA US Central Intelligence Agency, set up in 1947 to gather intelligence and conduct espionage in other countries.

Cold War Conflict between the USA and its allies and the Soviet Union and its allies, which lasted from 1945-1991.

Collective ownership Joint ownership of land or property for the benefit of all.

Communism Economic system which aims at abolishing private property and creating a classless society.

Ex-Comm Executive Committee of the National Security Council – the group of advisers assembled by Kennedy during the Cuban Missile Crisis.

Guerrilla A method of fighting a war using small mobile groups of fighters, acting independently. It comes from a Spanish word meaning 'little war'.

ICBM Intercontinental ballistic missile.

Marxist-Leninist Follower of the founding fathers of modern Communism: the German political theorist, Karl Marx, and the Russian revolutionary leader, Vladimir Ilyich Lenin.

MRBMs Medium-range ballistic missiles, with a range up to 1,700 km.

Nationalize Convert into nationally-owned property or land.

NATO North Atlantic Treaty Organization – a military alliance of western nations, headed by the USA, set up in 1949.

OAS Organization of American States. The OAS was set up by twenty-one American states in 1948, to settle disputes and strengthen the security of the Western hemisphere.

Polaris A submarine-launched ballistic missile.

Public relations Relations between an organization, or government, and the public.

Quarantine Isolating a person or place, usually for reasons of health e.g. to prevent disease spreading. The word has less military connotations than 'blockade'.

Radioactive Contaminated by the explosion of a nuclear bomb.

Resources

BOOKS

Robert F Kennedy *13 Days*
(Macmillan, 1968)
An emotional and dramatic account of
the crisis by the President's brother.
Currently available as a US paperback
(W W Norton and Co, 1999).

Nikita Khrushchev *Khrushchev Remembers*
(Sphere Books, 1971)
The Soviet leader's autobiography, with
his justification for installing the missiles,
and then withdrawing them. Now out of
print, but available in libraries.

E R May and P D Zelikov *The Kennedy
Tapes: Inside the White House During the
Cuban Missile Crisis* (Harvard Univerity
Press, 1977)
This book, with its transcripts of Ex-
Comm meetings, allows you to relive the
crisis as it unfolded, day by day, inside
the White House.

WEBSITES

14 Days in October: The Cuban Missile
Crisis. A lively interactive website on the
crisis:
http://library.thinkquest.org/11046/

NSA and the Cuban Missile Crisis
US National Security Archive of
documents:
www.nsa.gov/docs/cuba/archive.htm

Operation Mongoose: The PSYOPS
papers. CIA documents from the secret
war against Castro:
**http://parascope.com/ds/articles/
mongoosePSYOP.htm**

The Cold War
Comprehensive site accompanying the US
television series:
www.cnn.com/SPECIALS/cold.war/

Berlin Wall 1961
A well illustrated site on the Berlin Wall:
**http://www.dailysoft.com/berlinwall/
berlinwall_1961.htm**

QUOTATION SOURCES

Khrushchev Remembers by Nikita Khrushchev
(Sphere Books, 1971); *Kennedy v Khrushchev, The
Crisis Years* by Michael R Beschloss (Faber &
Faber, 1991); *The Brink: Cuba, Castro and John F
Kennedy, 1964* by David Detzer (J.M.Dent &
Sons, 1970); *Fidel Castro Speaks* edited by Martin
Kenner and James Petras, (Penguin, 1969);
Robert Kennedy and his Times by Arthur M.
Schlesinger Jnr (André Deutsch, 1978); *Eyeball to
Eyeball*, BBC2 television series Timewatch,
1992; *13 Days* by Robert F.Kennedy
(Macmillan, 1968); *The Kennedy Tapes: Inside the
White House during the Cuban Missile Crisis* edited
by E.R.May and P.D.Zelikow (Harvard
University Press, 1997); *On the Brink: Americans
and Soviets Re-examine the Cuban Missile Crisis* by
James G Blight and David Welch (Hill and
Wang, 1989); *As I Saw It* by Dean Rusk
(I.B.Tauris, 1991); *Back to the Brink: Proceedings of
the Moscow Conference on the Cuban Missile Crisis*
edited by B J Allen, J G Blight and D A Welch
(University Press of America, 1992); *We Now
Know: Rethinking Cold War History* by John Lewis
Gaddis (Oxford University Press, 1997); *The
Cuban Missile Crisis Revisited* edited by James
Nathan (St Martin's Press, 1992); *In Confidence*
by Anatoly Dobrynin (Times Books, 1995);
Venceremos! The Speeches and Writings of Che Guevara
edited by John Gerassi (Panther, 1972).

Index